TWENTIETH-CENTURY DEVELOPMENTS IN FASHION AND COSTUME

WOMEN'S COSTUMES

Other books in this series include:

Military Uniforms
Carol Harris and Mike Brown

Accessories
Carol Harris and Mike Brown

Children's Costumes
Carol Harris and Mike Brown

Men's Costumes
Carol Harris and Mike Brown

Festivals
Ellen Galford

North American Dress
Dr. Louise Aikman

Ceremonial Costumes
Lewis Lyons

Performing Arts
Alycen Mitchell

Everyday Dress
Chris McNab

Rescue Services
Carol Harris and Mike Brown

Religious Costumes
Ellen Galford

TWENTIETH-CENTURY DEVELOPMENTS IN FASHION AND COSTUME

WOMEN'S COSTUMES

CAROL HARRIS AND MIKE BROWN

MASON CREST PUBLISHERS

www.masoncrest.com

CHAPTER 1

The Early 1900s

Even at the beginning of the 20th century, when most women wore corsets, looser styles of dress were coming into fashion in styles and patterns not only encouraged by the Arts and Crafts and Art Nouveau movements, but also by the clothing worn by professional dancers.

It is difficult nowadays to comprehend the extent of the impact on fashion that the 1909 tour of the Ballets Russes (Russian Ballet) had. The Ballet Russes toured Europe, opening in Paris—the fashion capital of the world. Inspired by the colors

From the 1890s onward, the Gaiety Girl (right) typified the extravagant, hedonistic lives of women whose main occupation was socializing. Tight corsets (left) and large, elaborate hats, severely restricted movement.

9

and lines of the East, the Ballets Russes designers used fabulous fabrics and colors, and they were also influenced by the styles worn by Turkish women. The Ballets Russes designers were influential for years to come; their popularity was helped along by the fact that many settled in the United States and Europe after the Russian Revolution of 1917.

BEFORE THE WAR

As World War I loomed, fashionable middle-class women across Europe and the U.S. still changed their clothes several times a day—to take tea, have dinner, and go shopping. Needless to say, the lady's maid—whose duties consisted of helping her mistress to dress, and to launder and repair her wardrobe—was still indispensable. One of the most influential designers at this time was Lucile, who had branches of her own fashion house in London, New York, Paris, and Chicago between the years 1891–1918. Lucile was best known for her designs for Lily Elsie, star of the London stage hit *The Merry Widow,* for whom she made tea gowns and eveningwear.

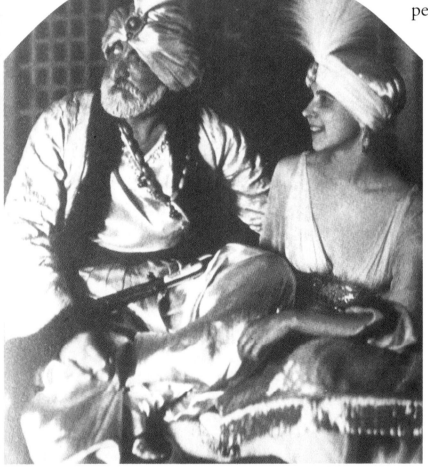

The craze for Eastern styling encouraged looser styles in dress and a trend for plumed headbands instead of more conventional hats.

DEPARTMENT STORES

Large and convenient, department stores thrived during World War I. The still-famous department store, Bloomingdale's, located in New York City, was among the first to have a small fashion department and to show selected clothes to invited audiences. At the time, department stores sold fabrics that customers could buy and have the store make into clothes. They also sold garments that were unfinished at the back, and thus could be fitted to the customer's figure.

PRACTICALITY

World War I had a substantial impact on fashion. The power of the fashion industry shifted temporarily from Paris to New York. Across Europe, wartime brought restrictions on the fabrics and trimmings available, and the rich and showy styles of the earlier part of the century were seen as unpatriotic. As casualties among the soldiers mounted, mourning clothes became less formal and more commonplace. Women volunteered to work in factories and offices and on buses, releasing men to fight. This meant that women no longer changed their clothes several times a day—one outfit would do. Moreover, the materials used were more practical than the silks, satins, and velvets that had been so popular during peacetime. Many women wore pants for the first time in their lives.

FROM PARIS TO NEW YORK

In direct fashion terms, World War I led to the creation of American **haute couture**. In the days before passenger aircraft, wealthy American women traveled on luxury liners across the Atlantic to Europe to buy the latest Paris fashions. During the war, however, German submarines were active in the Atlantic, which discouraged passengers from taking trips to Europe. Imports of

French fashions to the United States fell by half during this time. The fashion magazine *Vogue* reacted by organizing the first fashion show to feature the work of American designers. Sponsored by wealthy socialite Mrs. Henry Payne Whitney, the show traveled across the country.

INFORMAL STYLES

Immediately after World War I, attempts to revive the longer lengths and restrictive corsets of pre-war times were unsuccessful. The preferred shape for women until the '30s was a boyish, flat-chested look. Three Paris designers—Patou, Chanel, and Molyneux—concentrated on modern-looking **shift** styles, which were well received by younger women who wanted more relaxed and practical clothing to suit their lifestyles. Women also took to wearing separates and tailored suits, especially those in the new easy-to-wear fabrics such as knitted **jersey**. This informal style of suit was another innovation by the most influential designer of the time, Coco Chanel.

PANTS AND PAJAMAS

Women had worn pants while working in their wartime occupations. After the war, pants became a fashion item for women. Modern women also started wearing pajamas to bed in preference to nightgowns. There were a few different styles of pajamas, and each was worn for separate occasions: brightly colored silk or cotton versions for the evening; beach

Coco Chanel is wearing two typical Chanel innovations: the chic, two-piece suit and a string of pearls. Her bobbed hair was another feature of the relaxed and fluid styling of the 1920s.

Energetic dancing to the new jazz music meant that lacy underwear and decorative stocking tops were frequently on show.

pajamas for trips to the coast; and lounging pajamas for the home.

THE ROARING TWENTIES

In 1920, Prohibition outlawed the sale of alcohol across America. Despite its good intentions, this resulted in the growth of **speakeasies** and night-clubs, where people could drink alcohol illegally. Gangsters often owned and ran these establishments. During the decade known as the Roaring Twenties, the young people who enjoyed themselves so publicly were called the "bright young things," a name made popular by such authors as F. Scott Fitzgerald. Young women were called "flappers" or "jazz babies." The term "flapper" probably had its origins in the term "flapper bracket," the name for an active, sporty young woman who rode on the back of a motorcycle. "Jazz babies" danced in beaded dresses to the new jazz music, imitating the film star Clara Bow. Hemlines were at the ankle or calf for the first part of the 1920s, and they became progressively shorter until 1929, when hemlines started to become lower at the back and higher in the front.

CORSETS

The clothes worn by women at the start of the 20th century were evidence of the fact that their lives were fairly sedentary. During this time, fashion relied on an undergarment known as a corset. Made of whalebone and fabric, corsets were designed to make the waist unnaturally small by means of laces running down the garment that could be tightened to the desired size. Corseted ladies did not run or take part in any other exercise. Indeed, some women laced their corsets so tightly that they could hardly breathe.

During this time, the fashionable shapes for women's clothing were the **hourglass figure** and the **S-bend**, shapes made possible only by means of corsetry. The hourglass figure referred to a style of dress with padded hips and bust and a tight waist. In the S-bend style, the corset was cut low—to make the wearer's bottom stick out as she walked—and was shaped and tightened at the front to make the bust stick out.

CAMPAIGNING FOR COMFORT

Toward the end of the 19th century, a woman named Amelia Jenks Bloomer campaigned against corsets and for functional female clothing in her own feminist journal, *The Lily*. As a result, some women started wearing Turkish-style pants, or bloomers, as they became known in Mrs. Bloomer's honor. However, as the 20th century began, fashionable women still spent most of

The loose, harem-style trousers and the tiered skirts (right), as well as the smaller, more practical hats on all three models, are typical of the clothes worn before the outbreak of World War I.

their time in corsets, and the shapes of clothing styles were as unnatural and uncomfortable as ever. Underwear, however, was pretty, and was actually partially on display, because it was acceptable for lace and ribbon trimmings to be seen under dresses. Women wore camisole tops over their corsets, and knee-length cotton underpants with lace edgings and drawstring fastenings topped with layers of petticoats.

HOBBLE DRESSES

Campaigns against fashions based on health grounds had limited impact; instead, changing fashions were the key. In 1906, French designer Paul Poiret reduced the amount of underwear worn over corsets when he created a new, fashionable profile by slimming down the hips. The bust was still heavily padded, however, and the overall effect of this style—especially when worn with the fashionable "cartwheel" hats, so named because they were shaped like a large wheel—was definitely top-heavy. A few years later, in 1911, he revived the *directoire* style of Napoleonic France in dresses that flowed from just below a high bust to a narrow hem just above the ankle. These "hobble dresses," as they were known, still limited movement, but the corset was no longer needed to achieve the right body shape.

ANDROGYNY

Just after World War I, a boyish, or androgynous, look was in fashion, and so, thus, was underwear that flattened out the natural curves of the female form. Over the **chemise**, shapely women now wore the new "**foundation**" garment, sometimes called the combinaire. Invented in the United States, it became immensely popular because it was made from new, elasticized fabrics. The combinaire covered the body from the chest to the thighs, and was anchored in place by shoulder straps at the top and elastic suspenders at the bottom that also held up stockings.

STOCKINGS

Stockings were usually black in the daytime, but brightly colored and embroidered versions were also popular, especially for eveningwear. As the 1920s went on and legs became the focus of fashion, flesh colors also became popular. Stockings were made from wool, cotton, silk, and a new, artificial silk that was named **rayon** in a competition held in 1924.

BARE SKIN

By the mid-1920s, women wore as little as possible underneath their dresses, because bare skin was in fashion. The chemise became shorter and shorter until it developed into the modern vest, which was worn tucked into wide-legged knickers (underpants) that ended just above the knee. Long underpants were often elasticized around the leg. Camiknickers, combining a camisole top and knickers in one garment, might have just a thin strip of material buttoning between the legs. In the United States especially, pink, shiny artificial-silk stockings were worn just above the knee and rolled around garters made from elastic, fabric, or even metal.

HOLLYWOOD INFLUENCES

By the 1930s, Hollywood film stars and costume designers had become as influential on fashion as Paris had been before the war. Film magazines filled with beauty hints from the stars thrived, and actresses advertised makeup. Greta Garbo, Jean

The exotic turban, bright red lipstick, and wide shoulders of Hollywood actress Joan Crawford were widely copied in the 1930s.

BIAS CUTTING

Cutting a skirt or dress pattern diagonally, that is, in the direction of the grain of the cloth—known as bias cutting—became popular in the 1930s, especially for long evening dresses. While the skirt fitted closely around the hips, it fell in loosely draped folds at the hem. Bias cutting used about one-third more material than would otherwise be necessary, but the overall effect was one of fluid, smooth lines.

Harlow, and other Hollywood leading ladies modeled the Paris designers' new collections. Femininity was back, and women tried to look cool and sophisticated, in contrast to the exuberant sexuality of the 1920s "jazz babies." A suntan was an essential part of the active, sporty life.

Women took to wearing men's clothes, a trend Coco Chanel started in the early 1920s. Greta Garbo, Katharine Hepburn, and Marlene Dietrich made this look especially popular. Katharine Hepburn, in particular, wore pants in the male style—generously cut and with wide legs—and summed up the image of the young woman as sporty and independent. Women's pants fastened with a zipper up the side, instead of the front fly common to men's styles. Joan Crawford, with her bright red lipstick, was a more feminine but equally independent film star who also influenced fashion. Her trademark padded shoulders were a successful attempt by Hollywood costume designer Adrian to draw attention away from her wide hips.

DETAILS

Women's clothes in the 1930s were more detailed than they had been in the 1920s, with even simple garments featuring kick pleats, pin tucks, and trimmings. Heavily patterned or multicolored fabrics were popular, especially in the knitted jersey that

Chanel made popular. The new mass-produced plastics meant that buttons were often a highly decorative feature on a blouse or jacket. Knitting at home continued to be as popular as it was in the 1920s, and the range of yarns used was enormous: chenille, silk, artificial silk, and crepe were among the more exotic.

UNDERWEAR

By 1929, the preferred line for dresses was a soft curve from the shoulder to the waist. A gently curving bosom was fashionable, too, thus popularizing the elasticized bras with separate cups that we know today. The smooth lines created by bias-cut dresses demanded smooth and near-seamless underwear, and the solution was usually camiknickers. Camiknickers combined the flimsy camisole top of the corset days with underpants in a single garment. They were usually made in satin, silk, or artificial silk (also known as rayon). They were popular in the 1920s, along with variations on this theme, such as camibockers (a combination of camisoles and knickerbockers).

WORLD WAR II

In Europe, World War II limited the influence of Paris fashions, because the raw materials to make these fashions were simply not available during this time of scarcity. By contrast, the United States was "the land of plenty," and its styles in clothing, language, and culture were widely copied—especially when huge numbers of American soldiers (called GIs) arrived in Europe.

At home in the U.S., the government launched campaigns to preserve and recycle raw materials. From 1942 onward, clothes had to conform to the L-85 regulations. Among other limitations, the regulations banned wool linings and decorative pockets and flaps, but allowed decorations, such as fur, sequins, and braiding. Straight, Chinese-style dresses, sleeveless dinner gowns similar to those worn during World War I, and narrow pants were all popular styles that were still allowed under L-85. Some American designers, notably Magnin and

Falkenstein, produced uneven hemlines. Herbert Greer came up with the "long-short dress," in which the hem was 18 inches (45 cm) from the ground at the front, and 9 inches (22.5 cm) from the ground at the back. The American *Vogue* magazine estimated that L-85 led to savings of between 13 and 16 million yards (12 and 15 million m) of material.

Another result of the war was an emphasis on cotton—which was widely grown in the U.S.—and on synthetic fabrics. Because milk was not rationed, it was used to make a material called aralac, which was employed in the manufacture of overcoats. Limits on the sizes of coat collars made collarless coats fashionable. Women were told to shop to support the war effort, which they did with enthusiasm.

THE NEW LOOK

By the time World War II had ended, Europeans were tired of their old, much-mended clothes that had been designed for practicality and economy. Luxury

---

BRASSIERES

In 1914, Mary Phelps Jacobs took out the first patent for brassiere design. This early version was a garment made from two handkerchiefs and ribbon, and was the work of Ms. Jacobs and her maid. During the 1920s, brassieres were unshaped; as the idea was to flatten the chest, they did not usually have separate cups. Women with naturally small busts wore no brassiere at all. In the late 1920s, an American company called Kestos was among the first to produce the bra that we know today, with two triangles of fabric held in place by elastic. In the 1930s, the fashion for a shapelier bosom meant that the "bra," as it was known from then on, had achieved the form we recognize today. Moreover, bras were now, for the first time, made in different cup sizes.

was back "in," even if it was still only a dream (shortages continued in many parts of Europe). In fashion terms, this thirst for new and luxurious styling led to the most talked-about collection ever seen: Christian Dior's "Corelle Look," which he launched in 1947. These designs, which were eventually coined the "New Look" by American fashion editor Carmel Snow, picked up where the 1939 collections had been heading before they were interrupted by the war.

Dresses and suits were fastened with rows of tiny buttons. The curved and corseted shapes of the early 20th century were back, this time using lightweight, stretchy fabrics. French underpants were worn under full petticoats and topped with old-fashioned, lace-trimmed camisoles. However, the biggest controversy was caused by the new style of skirts, which were long, full, and required many yards of scarce material. Worn with high heels, the "New Look" was a sensation. Women everywhere wanted these wildly impractical garments. In Paris, however, the New Look caused such outrage that some women tore the clothes from the models as they walked down the street, and the House of Dior was picketed.

UNDERWEAR FABRIC

World War II made little difference to the main styles of lingerie, but it did make an enormous difference to the fabrics from which it was made. During the war, silk was in demand for parachutes and wool was neccessary for uniforms. Rubber (used in elastic) and metal (for fastenings) were also needed by the military.

This shortage of underwear fabric was remedied in part by the invention, in 1939, of a material called **nylon**, which was used to make stockings. As part of Dior's New Look, stockings—in nylon, but still with seams up the back—were held up by suspender belts made of elastic, nylon, and satin. All at once, extremely lightweight stockings were available—but only in the United States. In Europe, while everyone had heard of nylon stockings, no one could buy them in the shops. So when U.S. troops went to Europe, they made friends with the local women by giving out "nylons" as presents.

During the late 1940s and 1950s, American rock and roll music swept across the world, inspiring fashions as it did so. Young female fans wore huge skirts and yards of stiff petticoats or sweaters and tapered trousers.

These fashionable young women, pictured in Little Rock, Arkansas, in the 1950s, are each wearing several stiffened petticoats.

CHAPTER 2

1950–1969: A Fashion Revolution

Teenagers were an identifiable group in the United States ever since the 1940s. In the 1950s, however, American teen flicks and rock 'n' roll music inspired and encouraged teenage fashions across Europe, too.

Spanish designer Christobel Balenciaga loosened the waists of Dior's New Look and brought in the "semi-fitted" style, which involved a much straighter cut. Topper

Skirts and dresses became shorter and brighter (left). With short hair, long legs, and a flat chest, Twiggy (right) led the androgynous look of the 1960s.

coats—short coats that flowed out from the shoulder—were popular in the 1940s and early 1950s. Longer versions of this coat, known as swing, or tent, coats, allowed room for the fullest of skirts. Sheath dresses, with their small waists and tight skirts, were also popular.

PROM STYLE

Another important designer of the time was Pierre Balmain. Particularly influential in the United States, Balmain created dresses for younger women

with huge, full underskirts topped with **tulle** or lace. Teenage girls would wear these formal dresses to the high school prom with white gloves and their hair swept back off their faces.

SCREEN ICONS

During the 1950s, television was slowly becoming a part of most people's lives, but film stars were still the more glamorous trendsetters. Grace Kelly, Marilyn Monroe, and Audrey Hepburn were three very different 1950s screen icons, but each summed up a look of the decade. Kelly's image was of a cool, sophisticated woman; Monroe was the sexy and curvaceous "dumb blonde"; Hepburn was the **gamine**. Hepburn made her strongest

In *Sabrina*, Audrey Hepburn played the typical 1950s gamine as the chauffeur's young daughter who captures the hearts of two wealthy brothers.

fashion statement in the 1954 film *Sabrina,* in which she was dressed by a leading Paris designer of the 1950s, Hubert de Givenchy. In the film, she wore short, sculpted tops with cropped sleeves and **bateau necklines** that revealed her shoulders. Both on and off screen, Hepburn continued to wear Givenchy for many years afterward.

Women of all shapes and sizes had their fashion moment in the 1950s. If the boyish, gamine look was not her style, a woman had other choices—for example, she could go for the furs, curves, glitz, and outright glamour of Monroe or Elizabeth Taylor, who had made the transition from child star to adult actress by this time.

MARY QUANT

No matter what the style, most **ready-to-wear** clothes were, during the 1950s, cheaper versions of the haute couture of the Paris fashion houses. All this changed in the 1960s, however, when London designers, such as Mary Quant, began to design directly and only for the shops found in local shopping malls, where most people bought their clothes. Quant's clothes, which were aimed at younger women, were colorful and inexpensive. The '60s look of the miniskirt, the short *directoire*-line dress, the skinny rib sweater, and the **PVC** overcoat were all originally Quant's ideas.

Quant was immensely popular in the United States. On her first trip to New York, in 1959, fashion commentators, such as Sally Kirkland and Rosemary McMerture, welcomed her, and *Time* magazine ran a six-page article about her.

JACKIE KENNEDY

More formal fashions still had their champion, however, in Jackie Kennedy, the young and glamorous wife of U.S. president, John F. Kennedy. Jackie wore suits and matching pillbox hats in a style that combined the looks of Balenciaga and Chanel. The president's wife should, it was felt, favor an American designer,

CHAPTER 3

1970–2000: The Modern Woman

Fashion in the latter part of the 20th century reflected women's increasingly active lifestyles. Women worked in all types of jobs, and leisure time was often spent in exercise and sporting activities.

Fashion went to extremes in the 1970s. One example of extreme style was the maxi, a floor-length skirt or dress. This style was a reaction against the modern mini lengths of skirts and dresses during the space-age collections of the early to mid-1960s. Nostalgia and the anti-

This 1971 outfit (left) by John Bates shows how fashion was becoming silly. By the 1990s, as Vivienne Westwood's pantsuit (right) demonstrates, catwalk fashions only looked good on those with slender figures.

consumer ideas of the hippie movement encouraged the vogue for secondhand clothes and for old, rich fabrics, such as velvet and brocade. The ethnic styles of the East became even more popular than they had been in the 1960s. In addition, fashion knitting—part of the trend for making your own clothes and accessories—encouraged revivals of crochet, leather, macramé, and patchwork.

At the same time, major advances in clothing design came from several Japanese designers, such as Yamomoto, Yuki, and Kenzo. These designers specialized in creating draped, unstructured garments that flowed and wrapped around the body in ways never seen before.

DESIGNER DENIM

As jeans became popular with all age groups, denim became a fabric of fashion instead of just workwear, as it had been previously. However, denim was now dyed, patched, and artificially aged before it was made into dresses, skirts, and accessories. American styles were once

PUNK STYLE

In mid-1970s Britain, the punk movement was encouraging a much more aggressive style than was seen at this time in the United States. Its leading designer, Vivienne Westwood, was making waves with her **fetish**-based garments made from leather, rubber, and plastic. They were sold at "Sex," her shop on London's fashionable King's Road.

again setting fashion trends. Designers Ralph Lauren and Calvin Klein set international trends with their ready-to-wear collections. Klein's "designer" jeans were among the first brand names to challenge the classic Levi jeans. Ralph Lauren became famous in 1978 when he introduced his "Prairie Look." This was essentially a denim skirt worn in typical 1970s layered style over a white cotton petticoat. They were worn with a fringed buckskin jacket, a belt, and a full, softly romantic blouse.

WOMENS' FASHION MAGAZINES

Of all fashion magazines, *Vogue* was the 20th century's most influential. It began in 1892, but it did not become the leading fashion guide until the publishing company Condé Nast bought it in 1909. Condé Nast brought out an edition every two weeks, and was soon producing British, French, and Spanish editions, as well as an American one. In addition to the latest fashions, *Vogue* looked at society and the arts and featured leading graphic artists and photographers. Edna Woolman Chase, editor of *Vogue* and later, editor-in-chief from 1914–1952, encouraged the development of the American fashion industry. Diana Vreeland, a fashion writer who, for 30 years, told America what she thought was in good taste, eventually became editor, then editor-in-chief of *Vogue* from 1962–1971.

Harper's Bazaar magazine was the rival to *Vogue* for most of the century. Like *Vogue,* its comments on style were enhanced by its commitment to fashion design and photography. It was at its most influential from 1932 until 1958, when Carmel Snow was its editor.

Originally the trade journal for the clothing industry, *Women's Wear Daily* eventually became a popular magazine among the general public. This was due mainly to the efforts of John Fairchild, who became the magazine's publisher in 1960. *Women's Wear Daily* reported on not only fashion shows and trade gossip, but also on parties and charity balls. The magazine featured the works of innovative designers, artists, and photographers.

UNDERWEAR

The covered-up, layered look of the 1970s meant that underwear could be comfortable once again. Underpants made from nylon and other synthetic fabrics became less popular, because women discovered that cotton or cotton-based underpants were just as easy to wash, but were more hygienic to wear. Women had also learned from experience that nylon slips created static electricity that made dresses cling and ride up the legs, sparking and crackling as they did so. Tights were here to stay, but stockings made a comeback, too, this time with elasticized, lacy tops that held them up without the need for a separate garter belt. Bras with seam-free cups were also popular, especially for wearing under sweaters.

Camisoles and camiknickers, widely known as teddies, came back into fashion during the 1970s. These were made from **drip-dry** polyester, satin, or silk, and trimmed with lace. Matching ranges of camisoles, French underpants (with higher-cut legs than examples from earlier decades), briefs, and garters were sold in huge ranges of colors. The fitness boom of the 1970s and 1980s made practical underwear popular as well; the only women who still wore corsets had likely done so since the 1950s. A new and gentler generation of foundation garments was also now available. Underwear known as "body shapers" became a practical alternative to exercising to get women's bodies into the right shape.

The bustier top—shown in this 1998 outfit by Italian designers Dolce and Gabbana—is typical of the fashion popular in the late 1990s.

By the 1990s, underwear was taking its ideas from the sports industry. Sports bras, made from elastic fabrics, held the breasts comfortably in place and suited women's active lifestyles. This undergarment was often worn on its own, with nothing over it. This trend for underwear as outerwear started in the 1980s, when women wore thermal undershirts, and elaborately decorated 1950s-style **bustiers** became fashionable outerwear. This trend was given a real boost in the 1990s, when the French designer Jean-Paul Gaultier designed an outrageous gold bustier for pop star Madonna, which became popular and was imitated the world over.

During the last decade of the century, a fascination with the styles of previous decades brought back much of the underwear of those earlier times, although this time in synthetics such as Lycra, Elastane, and **spandex**. The Wonderbra™, designed in the 1950s in Canada, was relaunched at this time. This famous bra style started a trend for bras that—under various titles, such as "balcony" and "push-up" bras—shaped and enhanced the bosom. At the same time, underpants called "thongs" were also developed. An alternative to traditionally shaped underpants, the thong helped women avoid having visible panty lines under a clinging dress. Other women wore French underwear, and a brave few went without anything at all.

ROMANTICISM

At the beginning of the 1980s, punk style was followed by the "New Romantic" and "Gothic" styles (for teenagers anyway). In Britain, the wedding of the Prince of Wales and Lady Diana Spencer marked the arrival of another royal fashion icon. Lady Di, as the British tabloid press called her, was the fairytale princess who, at this stage, favored flowery dresses and demure prints.

GLITZ AND EXTRAVAGANCE

The 1980s was an age of affluence, typified by the extravagant style of Nancy Reagan, the wife of President Ronald Reagan. It was Nancy Reagan who

CHAPTER 4

Women's Sportswear

At the turn of the century, the middle-class women who dictated popular styles generally did not lead active lives. However, as younger middle-class women became more independent, this slowly began to change.

Access to university and college educations for women of the younger generation started to improve toward the end of the 19th century. This newly found freedom became part of a growing campaign for women to have equal opportunities in other areas of daily life, especially the domains of work and

The close-fitting bikini and one-piece costume (left) from 1963 are a sharp contrast to the looser and longer styles fashionable half a century earlier (right).

With her voluptuous figure, red hair, and long legs, film star Rita Hayworth was the typical 1940s sex symbol. This strapless bathing suit is made from the quicker-drying, close-fitting, synthetic materials that were widely used after the war.

interviews with the fashion press.

At this time, bathing suits were given an elegant makeover. Women no longer wore suits that covered their entire torsos, thighs, and upper arms; they wanted sleek, close-fitting swimwear that emphasized their figures. The new bathing suits were often made from wool or wool mixtures, and by today's standards were quite thick and bulky. Moreover, two-piece bathing suits at this time covered much more than today's "bikini" style. However, in the days before clinging synthetics, the bathing suits of the 1920s and 1930s were a huge advance on the voluminous designs that had been universal during the 19th century and early part of the 20th century. Another notable social change at this time was that mixed bathing became popular. This somewhat daring idea was explored in a popular song of the time called, "I Love To Go Swimming With Women."

In 1946, the bikini took swimwear to another level. Two Frenchmen launched a small, two-piece bathing suit—the bikini—at the same time. They were Louis Reard and the better-known sportswear designer, Jaques Heim. Heim originally called his creation the Atome, after the atom bomb. In the same year, however, the United States carried out atomic bomb tests on the Bikini Atoll in the South Pacific, and Heim's new costume became more commonly known as the "Bikini." Despite these early American connections, the bikini did not become popular in the U.S. until the mid-1960s.

OUT OF TOWN

Vacations in the country required a sportier wardrobe than usual, and women would pack clothes for walking, golf, or riding. From the 1920s onward, women no longer routinely rode sidesaddle. This meant that their clothing was similar to men's, although women preferred jodhpurs and ankle boots to the breeches and long riding boots men wore. Golfing skirts were short and deeply pleated, to allow for maximum movement. Some women copied men's styling in this sport, too, preferring to wear masculine tailored pants and practical waterproof jackets.

In the 1930s, the wealthy might have gone skiing at a fashionable resort in close-fitting jackets, weatherproof caps, and loose pants tucked into lace-up ski boots. Ski clothes were in muted colors and patterns, although skating dresses were brighter and shorter than ever

Corduroy shorts and short-length trousers were comfortable and practical everyday wear for women in the 1950s.

CHAPTER 5

Major Designers

Each decade of the 20th century has produced designers whose ideas have had a lasting impact, and as the decades have progressed, designer labels have increasingly dominated the global market for fashion.

PAUL POIRET (1900–1914)

Paul Poiret's first designs were for the Paris fashion house of Worth at the turn of the century. His career was helped along by the patronage of Rejane, a well-known actress of the time, and the American dancer Isadora Duncan. Poiret's main contributions to fashion were his clothing designs that needed

This Issy Miyake creation (left) from 1999 was "ready to wear," but only a few women were willing to spend a fortune on looking so ridiculous. It was the understated, tailored look (right) that sold well in the shops.

The body shape created by Paul Poiret's exotic, Eastern influenced styles (left) liberated women from corsets for decades, but his lampshade dresses (right) were a short-lived fashion.

no corsets. He was heavily influenced by the *directoire* style, with its low-cut dresses with high waistlines and puffy sleeves. He also drew from Japanese styling and from the costumes of the Ballet Russes. His fabrics were usually exotic and heavily colored, and they worked well with simple lines and shapes. His designs were often trimmed with exotic furs and scarves. In 1911, he created dresses in the *directoire*-style, with narrow, "hobble" skirts, which were worn without corsets. Two years later, he produced the "lampshade" dress, so-called because the hem of the tunic was wired to make it stand out. After World War I, his exotic styles were seen as old-fashioned.

HATTIE CARNEGIE (1918–1950s)

Hattie Carnegie launched her first collection in 1918, and she remained at the center of American fashion until her death in 1956. She produced her own ready-to-wear collections from the 1920s onward. During the 1930s and 1940s, she brought French designs to American women; she also made her mark with reserved, tailored suits and neat black dresses. Her salon in New York sold complete outfits, as well as lingerie and accessories. Many leading American designers worked for her at one time or another. During World War II, she was responsible for promoting American textiles and design. Her favorite design colors were black and a self-made shade she called "Carnegie Blue."

ADRIAN (1920s–EARLY 1940s)

Born Gilbert Adrian in Connecticut in 1903, the costume designer Adrian, as he was known during his adult life, had as much influence on fashion between 1926 and 1942 as the Parisian couturiers during this time. He went from Broadway to Hollywood, initially to design costumes for Rudolph Valentino, but in 1928, he became film studio MGM's chief costume designer, and soon he began to influence women's fashion. At that time, MGM boasted that it had "more stars than there are in heaven," and soon Adrian was making clothes for the leading actresses of the day; these designs were faithfully copied and worn by the women who went to see their films. Among Adrian's most famous creations was the slouch hat, which he designed for Greta Garbo; padded shoulders, which he fashioned for Joan Crawford; and slinky, bias-cut dresses, which he made for Jean Harlow (these dresses were so close-fitting it was rumored that she wore nothing underneath them).

Film actress Jean Harlow wears a slinky, bias-cut evening dress by Adrian in a photograph from the 1930s by George Hoyningen-Huene.

A PIONEER IN FASHION PHOTOGRAPHY

George Hoyningen-Huene was an early pioneer in fashion photography. After studying art and painting in Paris in the 1920s, he became chief photographer, first for *Vogue* magazine, then for *Harper's Bazaar* magazine, photographing leading actresses, such as Jean Harlow, in the latest Paris fashions. His style involved photographing models from above, and he often posed them in the style of ancient Greek statues. Having established himself as a world-class fashion photographer, he photographed many rich and famous celebrities.

COCO CHANEL (1920s–1930s; 1950s–1970s)

One of the most influential designers of the 20th century, Coco Chanel took over from Paul Poiret as the designer behind the next revolution in women's fashions. During World War I, she produced hats and simple, loose-fitting clothing, often using jersey fabrics, which, until then, had only been used for lingerie. She set the 1920s style for the short-haired, flat-chested, boyish female, and also, along with her arch-rival Patou, the feminine and elegant style of the 1930s. Chanel also reworked ideas from men's clothes to create clothes for women; examples of these innovative styles included berets, belted raincoats, bell-bottomed pants, and beach pajamas. Other Chanel creations included the "little black dress," collarless jackets and dresses, *bateau* necklines, large black bows, and plain outfits with heavy costume jewelry. Her comeback collection of suits and dresses, introduced in 1954, reestablished Chanel's style and popularity—especially in the United States—for the rest of the 20th century.

CLAIRE McCARDELL (1930s-1950s)

Claire McCardell was one of the most influential American designers of the 20th century. Born in Maryland, she started designing in the early 1930s for Townley

Frocks. There, her most successful contribution was the "monastic dress," a bias-cut, tent-shaped dress worn with a belt. Her favorite fabrics were cotton, gingham, denim, and jersey, and her designs were all about practical, easy-to-wear clothes for active women. Patch pockets, rivets, and deep armholes were typical McCardell touches. In the 1940s, she produced the "Future Dress," made from two triangles of fabric that were belted and tied at the neck, and the wraparound dress. In the 1950s, when simpler lines were replacing those of Christian Dior's New Look, McCardell's styles became influential across Europe.

CHRISTIAN DIOR (1940s–1950s)

Dior set the style of the post-war 1940s and 1950s with the "Corelle Look," more popularly known as the "New Look." Elements of the New Look had already been glimpsed in the collections of late 1939, but the 1947 version shocked Europe, where wartime had meant making do with and mending old garments. The New Look style—which included tightened waists; huge, full, ankle-length skirts; and shaped busts—meant the return of the corset. Layers of stiff petticoats and the new "**waspie**" (a shortened corset) were essential lingerie. Dior continued to set trends until his death in 1957. This was also the year in which he launched his "Young Collection," a range of luxury casual sports clothes that was enormously

This model shows how, by 1954, Christian Dior had softened his New Look. Her heavily patterned dress still has the full skirt and tight waist that he featured seven years before. The long gloves are typical of 1950s style.

popular in the United States. After his death, his protégé Yves Saint Laurent took over his design house, and the Dior name continued to be a fashion leader.

CHARLES JAMES (1940s–1950s)

Fashion designers are often known for being talented but temperamental. Even so, Charles James stood out as both a genius and an appalling businessman with a terrible temper. James regarded his creations as sculptures, routinely disregarding schedules and budgets as he repeatedly took his designs apart and rebuilt them until he was satisfied. He worked mainly in New York, where his clients were the leading American socialites of the 1940s and 1950s. Today, his influence can still be seen in design and fashion museums all over the world. Among his enduring ideas were spiral shapes achieved carefully by drapery, luxurious fabrics, and prominent lapels.

GEOFFREY BEENE (1950s–1960s)

A major fashion influence in the second half of the 20th century, Geoffrey Beene trained and worked in Paris in the late 1940s and early 1950s, where he was influential in the domain of ready-to-wear clothes. In the early 1960s, he set up his own company in New York. Geoffrey Beene's influence over other designers has been wide-ranging, but he was especially well known in the early 1960s for his range of empire-line dresses. Typical Beene style features sensual combinations of fabrics, fantasy, fine detail, and geometric cut and decoration.

MARY QUANT (1960s)

The designer most associated with "Swinging London," as London was known then, Quant's fashion revolution involved designing ready-to-wear clothes that set the style for haute couture design, reversing the usual approach. Colored tights, skinny-rib sweaters, and most famously of all, the miniskirt, were all Quant innovations. Enormously successful in JC Penny

British fashion designer Mary Quant is holding a copy of a French edition of *Vogue*, featuring on its cover another 1960s icon, the model Twiggy.

stores, Quant also designed for the Puritan Fashions Group, and later specialized in knitwear.

BILL BLASS (1960s–1970s)

Bill Blass initially made his name with exuberant daywear, and his designs still often feature small splashes of bright colors, as well as ruffles. One of his most popular designs in the late 1960s was a beige lace dress with a ruffled collar and cuffs, worn and made famous in 1968 by model Jean Shrimpton.

RALPH LAUREN (1960s–1970s)

Ralph Lauren's famous "Polo" range of separates started in 1967 with a collection of wide, handmade ties. He launched his own label in 1972, and produced women's collections of casual, tailored separates in cashmere and tweed. Fair Isle patterns, velvet dresses, and flannel pants were also an established part of his style. Lauren effectively invented the classic American style with these, as well as his "Prairie" and "Frontier" looks, which were based on traditional American costumes of the 19th century.

1968 Neil Armstrong is the first man to walk on the moon.

1970s Another economic crisis hits the Western world; secondhand clothing and retrospective styles in new fashions reflect uncertainty about the future; fitness boom creates a trend for clothes originally worn by dancers in rehearsal.

1980 Flash and brash is the style as First Lady Nancy Reagan revives the sheath dress, and soap operas such as *Dallas* and *Dynasty* set trends for looking like a million dollars.

1990s As the century draws to a close, retro is the style, with fashions of almost every preceding decade enjoying revivals.

FURTHER INFORMATION

BOOKS

Ashelford, Jane. *The Art of Dress: Clothes and Society, 1500–1914.* New York: Harry N. Abrams, 1996.

Caldwell, Doreen. *And All Was Revealed: Ladies Underwear 1907–1980.* London: Arthur Barker, 1981.

Clancy, Deirdre. *Costume Since 1945.* London: Herbert Press, 1996.

Evans, Caroline and Minna Thornton. *Women and Fashion.* London: Quartet, 1989.

Ewing, Elizabeth. *History of 20th Century Fashion (revised edition).* New York: Quite Specific Media Group Ltd., 2002.

Harris, Carol. *Miller's Collecting Twentieth-Century Fashion and Accessories.* London: Mitchell Beazley, 2000.

Mulvagh, Jane. *Vogue History of Twentieth-Century Fashion.* London: Viking, 1988.

O'Hara Callan, Georgina. *Dictionary of Fashion and Fashion Designers.* London: Thames and Hudson, 1998.

Polhemus, Ted. *Streetstyle.* London: Thames and Hudson, 1994.

Robinson, Julian. *Fashion in the '30s.* London: Oresko Books, 1978.

Schmidt, Clara (Trans. William Wheeler). *Costumes.* Paris, France: Aventurine, 2002.

Watt, Judith, ed. *The Penguin Book of Twentieth-Century Fashion Writing.* London: Viking, 1999.

ONLINE SOURCES

The Costume Gallery

www.costumegallery.com

Research 20th-century fashions with this site, which specializes in pictures and information on women's changing fashions throughout the decades.

Museum of Costume

www.museumofcostume.co.uk

For 20th-century fashion, go to "Highlights,, then "Dress Since 1900." Also includes the Dress of the Year collection: each year since 1963, a fashion expert has selected an outfit for the museum's collection to represent the most important new ideas in contemporary fashion.

Vogue and *W* magazines

www.style.com

The online site for these women's magazines, with links to many others. You can search for fashion shows by designer, or by season.

20th-Century Design—Ethnic Influences

http://udel.edu/~orzada/toc.htm

This University of Delaware site provides extensive information and illustrations on ethnic influences on 20th-century fashion.

ABOUT THE AUTHORS

Mike Brown lives in London, England, where he writes and teaches part-time, in addition to giving talks and lectures on 20th-century history and architecture. He has written several books about everyday life during World War II: *Put That Light Out* (Sutton, 1999), *A Child's War* (Sutton, 2000), and, with his wife, Carol Harris, *The Wartime House* (Sutton, 2000).

Carol Harris is a freelance journalist specializing in the 1920s, '30s, and '40s. She has contributed to exhibitions at the Imperial War Museum on wartime fashions and utility clothing, and regularly gives talks on these and related topics. Other books include *Collecting Twentieth-Century Fashion and Accessories* (Mitchell Beazley 1999), and *Women at War—in Uniform* (Sutton, 2002).

INDEX